If you like this book you might also want to read *Knock Knocks, The Most Ever* by William Cole (in a Laurel-Leaf edition).

THE LAUREL-LEAF LIBRARY brings together under a single imprint outstanding works of fiction and non-fiction particularly suitable for young adult readers, both in and out of the classroom. The series is under the editorship of Charles F. Reasoner, Professor of Elementary Education, New York University.

Riddles and Fun for Everyone

The
Six-Million-Dollar
CUCUMBER

COMPILED BY
E. RICHARD CHURCHILL

PICTURES BY
CAROL NICKLAUS

LAUREL-LEAF
LIBRARY

Published by
Dell Publishing Co., Inc.
1 Dag Hammarskjold Plaza
New York, New York 10017

Text copyright © 1976 by E. Richard Churchill
Illustrations copyright © 1976 by Carol Nicklaus

ISBN: 0-440-97973-0

Reprinted by arrangement with Franklin Watts, Inc.
Printed in the United States of America
First Laurel-Leaf printing May 1977

Contents

For all boys and girls who enjoy riddles,
but especially for the students of
Billie Martinez Elementary School
and Maplewood Middle School,
Greeley, Colorado

The Six-Million-Dollar Cucumber

$6,000,000

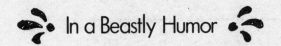 In a Beastly Humor

Why did Santa have only
seven reindeer on Christmas Eve?

> Comet was home cleaning the sink.

•

What do teen-age boy gorillas do when
they see pretty teen-age girl gorillas?

> They go ape.

•

What did the beaver say to the tree?

> It's been nice gnawing you.

•

If a skunk got its nose cut off,
how would it smell?

> As bad as ever.

•

What should you do if you find
a gorilla asleep in your bed?

> Sleep somewhere else.

What did the baby porcupine say
when he backed into a cactus?

Is that you, Mother?

•

What is gray, has four legs, and
weighs ninety-eight pounds?

A fat mouse.

•

How do you move in a crowd of porcupines?

Very carefully.

•

Why will 1980, 1984, and 1988
be good years for kangaroos?

They are leap years.

•

What animal eats with its tail?

All animals do.
They also sleep with them.

•

Who is safe when a man-eating tiger is loose?

Women and children.

What is the highest form of animal life?

A giraffe.

•

Why are leopards spotted?

So you can tell them from fleas.

•

What makes more noise than an angry lion?

Two angry lions.

•

What do hippopotamuses have
that no other animals have?

Baby hippos.

•

Where do you find tigers?

It depends upon where they were lost.

•

What would you get if you crossed
a laughing hyena and a cat?

A giggle puss.

What place of business helps animals
who have lost their tails?

A retail store.

•

Is it better to have a
lion eat you, or a tiger?

It is better to have him eat the tiger.

•

Why did the kangaroo go to the doctor?

He wasn't feeling jumpy anymore.

•

How do you get fur from a bear?

Run fast in the opposite direction.

•

What animals should carry an oilcan?

Mice. They squeak.

•

How can you stop
a buffalo from charging?

Take away his credit card.

What did the leopard say
after he had eaten the hunter?

That sure hit the spot.

•

What should you do
if you see an angry rhino?

Hope he doesn't see you.

•

Why do giraffes have such long necks?

To connect their
heads to their bodies.

•

What is worse than a
giraffe with a sore throat?

A centipede with fallen arches.

•

A zebra with wide stripes married
a zebra with narrow stripes.
Their first son had no stripes.
What did they call him?

Howard.

What must a lion tamer know
to teach a lion tricks?

More than the lion.

•

What animal is like a tailor?

The porcupine.
It has thousands of needles.

•

Why are wolves like cards?

They come in packs.

•

What would you get if you
crossed a porcupine and a skunk?

A smelly pincushion.

•

Why is it so cheap to feed a giraffe?

A little goes a long way.

•

When is a boy like a bear?

When he goes barefoot.

Why did King Kong climb
the Washington Monument?

To get his kite.

•

What animal is the
best baseball player?

The bat.

•

What is a monkey that
eats potato chips called?

A chip monk.

•

A man got a thousand-pound
gorilla for a pet.
Where did the gorilla sleep?

Wherever he wanted to.

•

How can you keep
a skunk from smelling?

By holding his nose.

❧ From the Funny Farm ❧

How can you recognize rabbit stew?

It has some hares in it.

•

What did the goat say
when he ate a reel of film?

The book was better.

•

What is the best medicine
for a pig with a sprained ankle?

Oinkment.

•

Which horses have six legs?

All of them. They have forelegs
in the front and two in the back.

•

What is an Eskimo cow?

An Eskimoo.

What did the dude say
after his first horseback ride?

I never knew anything
stuffed with hay could be so hard.

•

Why did the farmer
feed his sheep chunks of steel?

He wanted them
to grow steel wool.

•

Why did the little pig
eat such a big meal?

He was making a hog of himself.

•

When is a pig like ink?

When it is in a pen.

•

What eats hay and
sees as well from either end?

A horse with its eyes shut.

When is it proper to
go to bed with your shoes on?

When you are a horse.

●

What animals are always with you?

A pair of calves.

●

What animal has the poorest manners?

The goat. It is always butting in.

●

What did the horse say to the pig?

You are just a boar.

●

Why did the farmer's horse
go over the mountain?

He couldn't go under it.

●

What cow is an article of clothing?

A Jersey.

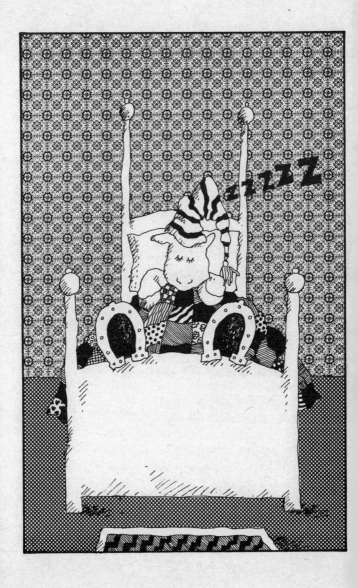

Why are barns so noisy?

    The cows have horns.

•

What horse is found only at night?

    A nightmare.

•

What is a sleeping bull called?

    A bulldozer.

•

How is a sucker like a racehorse?

    The more you lick it,
    the faster it goes.

•

What animal is a tattletale?

    The pig always
    squeals on you.

•

When is a horse not a horse?

    When he turns into a barn.

What would you put on a horse
that is going out at night?

A satellite.

●

Why couldn't the pony talk?

He was a little horse.

●

Why did the boy
stand behind the donkey?

He thought he would
get a kick out of it.

●

What did Paul Revere
say to his horse at the
end of his historic ride?

Whoa.

●

How are an egg
and a horse alike?

They must be broken
before using.

🐾 Dogs and Cats Are Funny Folks 🐾

Where was the yellow cat
when the lights went out?

> In the dark.

•

What do you call a dog that sticks
his right paw down a lion's throat?

> Lefty.

•

Why is a dog like a baseball player?

> He runs for home when
> he sees the catcher coming.

•

Why does a dog wag his tail?

> Nobody will wag it for him.

•

How are a dog and a flea different?

> A dog can have fleas,
> but a flea can't have dogs.

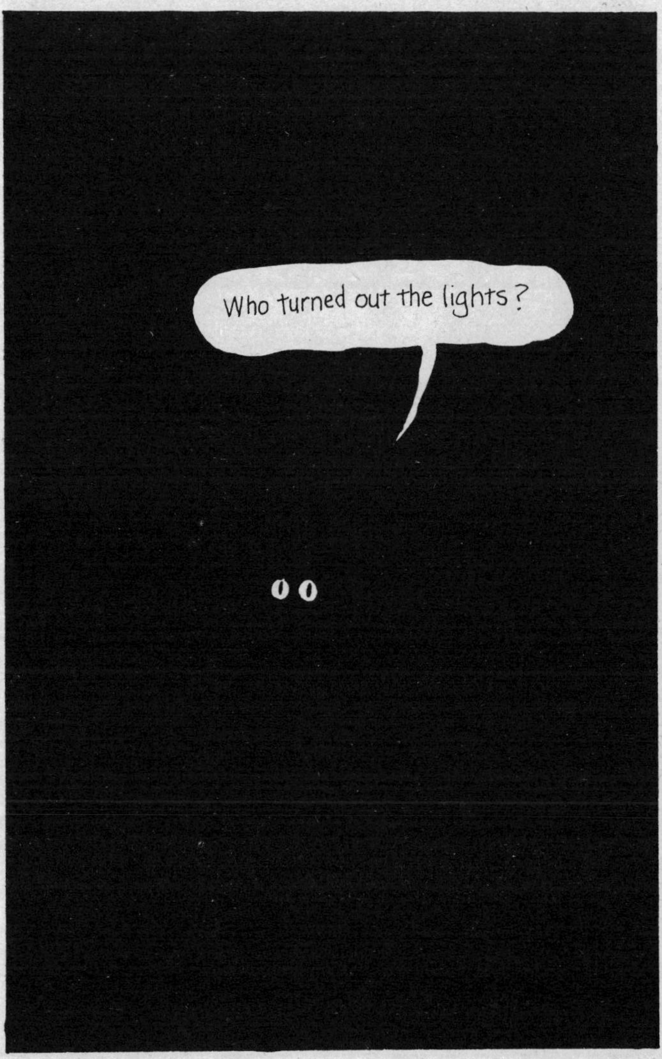
Who turned out the lights?

Get the POINT?
HA HA HoHoHoHeHeHaHa Ho HoHa
HA HA HA HoHoHo HeHe HEEE

What dog is impolite?

　　The pointer.

●

What would you call a small black cat
in Russia if it was ten days old and
had a white spot on the end of its nose?

　　A kitten.

●

Why did the mother
buy her six children a dachshund?

　　She wanted a dog
　　they could all pet at once.

●

If five dogs are chasing a cat
down the street, what time is it?

　　Five after one.

●

How can you stop a dog
from barking in the backyard?

　　Put him in the front yard.

Why didn't it do any good
to put an ad in the paper
when Joe lost his dog?

Joe's dog never
reads the paper.

•

What did the dog say
as he chased his tail?

This is the end.

•

If your cat ate a lemon,
what would she become?

A sourpuss.

•

When is it bad luck to have
a black cat cross your path?

When you are a mouse.

•

Which side of a cat has the most fur?

The outside.

What weather do mice most dislike?

   When it rains cats and dogs.

●

When is it proper to
drink your milk from a saucer?

   When you are a cat.

●

What should you do with a dog
who is eating a dictionary?

   Take the words right out of his mouth.

●

Why did the dog run in circles?

   He was a watchdog and needed winding.

●

What did the dog do at the flea circus?

   He stole the show.

●

Why are cats such gossips?

   They always carry tails with them.

What dog is
without a tail?

A hot dog.

•

What do you get
when you cross a dog
with a chicken?

A hen that lays
pooched eggs.

•

How are a dog and
a penny alike?

Both have a
head and a tail.

•

How are a cat and
a comma different?

A cat has claws at the
end of its paws, but
a comma has a pause
at the end of its clause.

Elephants Are Nice Too

How can you tell if
an elephant is under your bed?

> You can touch the ceiling
> with your nose.

•

How do you scold an elephant?

> Say tusk tusk.

•

How can you tell
an elephant from a professor?

> The elephant remembers.

•

What time is it when
an elephant sits on your car?

> Time to buy a new car.

•

What has four legs but can't walk?

> A dead elephant.

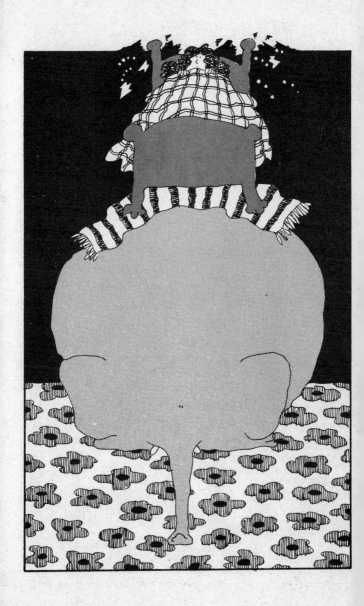

When twelve elephants
fall into a lake, what is
the first thing they do?

Get wet.

●

What has eight legs but can't walk?

Two dead elephants.

●

What did the elephant do
when he broke his toe?

He called a tow truck.

●

Why did the elephant leave the zoo?

He was tired of
working for peanuts.

●

How can you tell an
elephant from spaghetti?

An elephant doesn't
slip off the end of your fork.

How can you keep an
elephant from smelling?

> Tie a knot in its trunk.

●

How do you get a napkin
from under an elephant?

> Wait for the elephant to get up.

●

Why is an elephant huge,
gray, and wrinkled?

> So you can tell him from an aspirin.

●

How do you get down
from an elephant?

> You get down from
> ducks or geese, not elephants.

●

What is the difference between
an elephant and a grapefruit?

> An elephant is gray.

What is gray, has a trunk,
has big ears, and weighs ten pounds?

    A very thin elephant.

•

How long should
an elephant's legs be?

    Long enough to
    reach the ground.

•

Why do elephants eat mothballs?

    To keep moths out of their trunks.

•

The elephant fell off
a hundred-foot ladder
but wasn't hurt. Why?

    He fell from the bottom rung.

•

Why does an elephant
have wrinkled knees?

    From scrubbing floors.

How are an elephant
and a VW alike?

They both have
a trunk in front.

•

Why do elephants have ivory tusks?

Iron ones would rust.

•

Why do elephants lie down?

They can't lie up.

•

Why don't elephants ride tricycles?

They don't have a thumb
to ring the bell.

•

How can you best hide an elephant?

Skin him.

•

Why are elephants poor dancers?

They have two left feet.

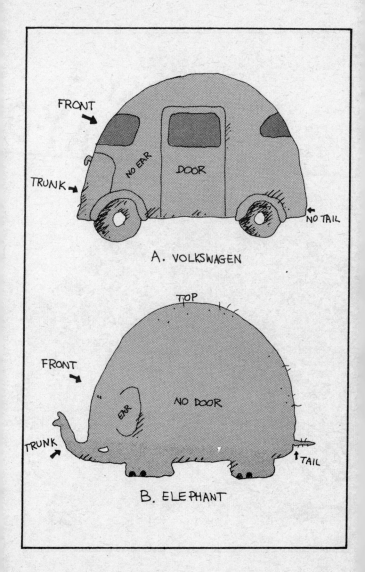

A. VOLKSWAGEN

B. ELEPHANT

What weighs two tons and sings?

> Harry Elafonte.

•

Why don't elephants
play basketball?

> They can't buy
> round sneakers.

•

When can you see
an elephant in
a box of popcorn?

> Never. They come
> in Cracker Jacks.

•

Why did the elephant
put his trunk across the trail?

> To trip ants.

•

Why do elephants have trunks?

> They would look silly
> with glove compartments.

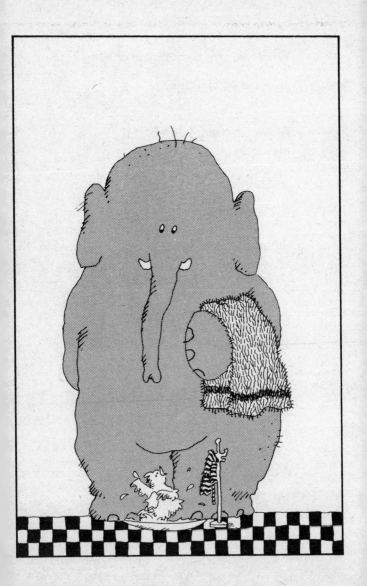

✈ High Flyers ✦

What can a canary do
that an elephant can't?

Take a bath in a saucer.

●

What is yellow, sings,
and has twenty-four legs?

A dozen canaries.

●

How are a goose and a car alike?

They both honk.

●

What happens to a duck
that flies upside down?

He is apt to quack up.

●

What would you get if you crossed
a hummingbird and a doorbell?

A humdinger.

Why did the hen stop
in the middle of the highway?

> She wanted to lay it on the line.

•

Why was the young owl
doing so poorly in school?

> He didn't seem to care
> a hoot about anything.

•

Who is never hungry on Thanksgiving?

> The turkey. He is stuffed.

•

How can a farmer spot a frightened crow?

> When it brings back the
> corn it stole last year.

•

Why was the hen sitting on the sofa?

> She heard some men were going
> to lay a carpet and she
> wanted to see how they did it.

What is the strongest bird?

> The crane. It can pick up a car.

●

Where do giant condors come from?

> Eggs.

●

Why do hummingbirds hum?

> They didn't learn the words.

●

When is a turkey like a ghost?

> When he is a-gobblin'.

●

What sort of story
did the peacock tell?

> A big tale.

●

What did the pelican say
when he caught a large fish?

> This sure fills the bill.

What bird is always with you at lunch?

A swallow.

•

What is a smart duck?

A wise quacker.

•

What kind of hawk has no wings?

A tomahawk.

•

What do you call a bird that
got caught in the lawnmower?

Shredded tweet.

•

What do you get when you
cross an owl and a goat?

A hootenanny.

•

An egg was on a plate in New York City.
Where did it come from?

A hen.

Creepy Crawlers

What is a caterpillar?

An upholstered worm.

•

What animal didn't enter
the ark in pairs?

Worms came in apples.

•

What snake stretches?

A garter snake.

•

What snake is best at arithmetic?

The adder.

•

Why did the mother flea
feel so terrible?

All her children
had gone to the dogs.

What's worse than
a snake with sore ribs?

A centipede
with athlete's foot.

•

What was the turtle
doing on the freeway?

About half a mile an hour.

•

What did the mother lightning bug
say to her son's teacher?

Isn't he bright for his age!

•

When insects take a trip,
how do they travel?

They go for a buggy ride.

•

Why did the moth
eat holes in the carpet?

It wanted to see
the floor show.

Why did the ants
run along the cracker box?

> The instructions said
> "Tear along the dotted line."

•

What is the best thing for hives?

> Bees.

•

What do bees do with honey?

> Cell it.

•

What animal is smartest?

> Ants. They can
> always find you when
> you go on a picnic.

•

What wears a cape,
flies through the air,
and fights crime?

> Super Mosquito.

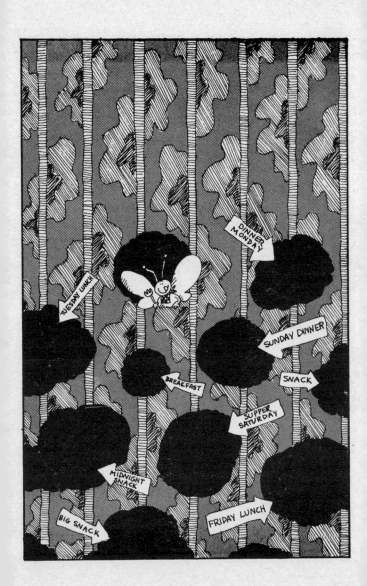

What animal eats the least?

A moth. It eats holes.

●

What is the smallest skin diver?

A mosquito.

●

Which snake is richest?

The diamondback rattler.

●

What insect is a
good baseball player?

The spider. It catches flies.

●

What is smaller
than a flea's mouth?

A flea's lips.

●

What is a mosquito?

A flying hypodermic needle.

✪✪✪ Fishy Doings ✪✪✪

What does a teen-age boy octopus
say to a teen-age girl octopus?

> Let me hold your hand, hand, hand,
> hand, hand, hand, hand, hand.

•

How are a tuna fish
and a piano different?

> You can't tune a fish.

•

What is a goldfish?

> A wet pet.

•

Where does a jellyfish get its jelly?

> From the ocean's currents.

•

What did the lobster say when
he was being taken home for dinner?

> I've already eaten.

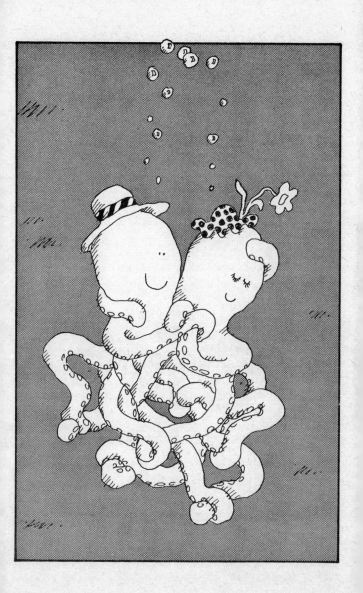

What fish is in a birdcage?

The perch.

●

Why did the fish swim across the lake?

He couldn't walk around it.

●

What did one large pike say to another?

Nothing. He had a frog in his throat.

●

Why did the restaurant serve crabs?

They serve everyone, crabby or not.

●

What fish is served on bread?

A jellyfish.

●

Why is an octopus a good fighter?

He is always well armed.

●

What fish is always surprised?

A fluke.

What fish is man's best friend?

> The dogfish.

•

Did you ever see a catfish?

> No, but I saw a horsefly.

•

What creature is best seen at night?

> A starfish.

•

Why didn't the little boy
give his goldfish fresh water?

> They hadn't finished the water
> he gave them last week.

•

What fish goes boating?

> A sailfish.

•

What animals are weight watchers?

> Fish. They carry their scales
> with them all the time.

 This Beets Everything

Why did the boy put dirt in his shoes?

He wanted his corns to grow.

•

Why did the man have to
go to the hospital after a
tomato fell on his head?

It was in a can.

•

What did one sugar beet
say to the other sugar beet?

Take me to your weeder.

•

Why did the farmer go over
his field with a steamroller?

He wanted to raise mashed potatoes.

•

What is green and goes putt, putt?

An outboard pickle.

What is green, has one
bionic eye, and fights crime?

    The Six-Million-Dollar Cucumber.

•

Where did the
baby ear of corn come from?

    The stalk brought him.

•

When does an Irish potato
come from another country?

    When it is french-fried.

•

If you raise corn in
dry weather, what do you
raise in wet weather?

    An umbrella.

•

Why was the cornstalk
angry with the farmer?

    The farmer kept pulling its ears.

What stays hot even though it is cold?

    Pepper.

●

Why didn't the little boy eat
his spinach after his mother told him
it would put color in his cheeks?

    He didn't want green cheeks.

●

If you take off my skin I won't cry,
but you will. Who am I?

    An onion.

●

How do you turn a
watermelon into a squash?

    Drop it from a third-floor window.
    It will squash when it hits the ground.

●

Why was the farmer
taken to jail this morning?

    He hit the hay last night.

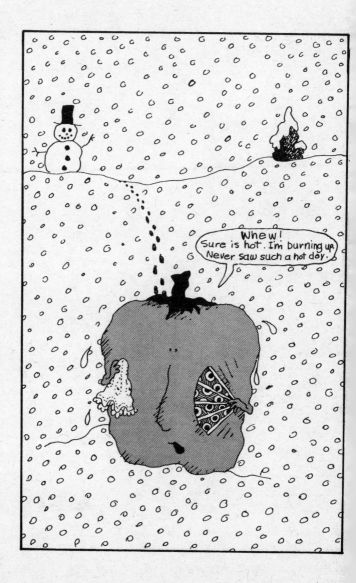

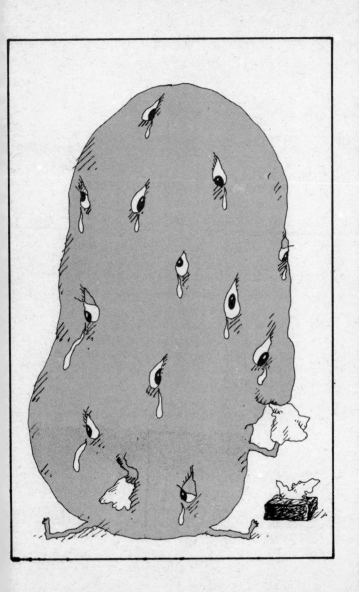

What do you get if you
cross a potato with an onion?

A potato with watery eyes.

●

Why does a watermelon
contain so much water?

It was planted in the spring.

●

What vegetables are
always found in a piece of music?

Beets.

●

What is green, then purple,
then green, then purple?

A pickle that works
part-time as a grape.

●

What room has no walls,
no doors, and no windows?

A mushroom.

What plant is sharpest?

> Grass. It grows as a blade.

•

How can you raise a salad?

> With a fork.

•

What beans won't grow from seeds?

> Jelly beans.

•

How many onions can you
put into an empty sack?

> One. After that
> the sack is no longer empty.

•

What is the best way to keep lettuce?

> Don't return it.

•

How do you make gold soup?

> Put in fourteen carrots.

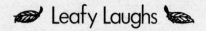 Leafy Laughs

What's red and goes beep beep?

A strawberry in a traffic jam.

•

What's purple and
lives in Minneapolis?

Mary Tyler Plum.

•

What flower did Lassie wear?

A collie flower.

•

What is made
from banana peels?

Slippers.

•

What tree can you
carry in your hand?

A palm.

What would the little boy have
who gave five apples to Nancy
and five apples to Martha?

Two new girl friends.

●

What is a raisin?

A worried grape.

●

What did one grape
say to another grape?

Nothing. Grapes can't talk.

●

Why was the detective
suspicious of the petunias?

She found them
in a garden plot.

●

What flowers grow
between your chin and nose?

Tulips.

What is red and dangerous?

A herd of stampeding apples.

•

What's green and makes loans?

First National City Pickle.

•

How can you recognize
a dogwood tree?

By its bark.

•

Did you ever seen a lemon peel?

No, but I saw a clam bake.

•

What nut might you
hang a picture on?

A walnut.

•

What fruit is on coins?

The date.

What is the best thing
to put into an apple pie?

Your teeth.

•

What nut is found
by the sea?

The beechnut.

•

What's yellow
and flickers?

A lemon with a
loose connection.

•

What is the most
dangerous flower?

The tiger lily.

•

What fruit is found
in light bulbs?

A currant.

About the Author

E. Richard Churchill is a librarian for the Maplewood Middle School in Greeley, Colorado. For the past seventeen years he has worked as both a teacher and a librarian. This experience with children has made him particularly partial to riddles as a source of fun and reading success. Mr. Churchill has over fifteen books to his credit, including *Fun with American History* (Abingdon) and *Puzzle It Out* (Scholastic). *The Six-Million-Dollar Cucumber* was compiled with the help of his two sons, Eric and Sean.

About the Artist

Carol Nicklaus is an illustrator and animation designer whose works include over two dozen children's books and short films for NBC–TV and *Sesame Street*. She has illustrated *The Sesame Street Coloring Book; Letters, Sounds and Words; Hugh and Fitzhugh;* and *Let's Find Out About Water;* and she has written and illustrated four books for children. She is a designer on the feature-length animated film *Raggedy Ann and Andy,* scheduled for release in September 1976.

Carol lives in Danbury, Connecticut, with her husband, Eric; dog Daniel the Spaniel; and eighteen-year-old, eighteen-pound cat Rusty. She is an experienced sailor and average autoharp player.